*"Our Humanity@Work"*

Working with the 7Cs – the 7 Human Capacities –
for Insight, Learning and Change

A NEW LENS FOR COACHING, COACHING SUPERVISION
AND EXECUTIVE REFLECTION

Reflective Practice Workbook and Journal
Elaine Patterson

Welcome!

Welcome to *"Our Humanity@Work"*
Working with the 7Cs – the 7 Human Capacities – for Insight, Learning and Change
A New Lens for Coaching, Coaching Supervision and Executive Reflection

This Workbook has been designed to introduce you to the 7Cs, and to give you – and your clients – a structure to capture your insights, reflections, learning and next steps.

*Section 1:*     The Bigger Picture
*Section 2:*     Origins of the 7Cs
*Section 3:*     Defining the 7Cs
*Section 4:*     Working with the 7Cs
*Section 5:*     Self-Assessment Map
*Section 6:*     7Cs in Action
*Section 7:*     References, Further Resources and Reading

A set of cards has also been designed to support this Workbook and are available by emailing me.

I would love to hear about your experience of using the 7Cs in your life and work. Please email me at elaine@ep-ec.com with thoughts, feedforward and further refinements.

I shall look forward to hearing from you.

> Life is a long journey between human being and being human.
> Let's take at least one step each day to cover the distance.
>
> Wordion

# Section 1
## The Bigger Picture

# Section 1
## The Bigger Picture

I have developed the 7Cs as a new lens for Coaching, Supervision and Executive Reflection in response to what I have been noticing in myself, my clients and from my research over recent years[1].

The 7Cs is a new lens for Coaching, Supervision and Executive Reflection which works alongside existing models and processes whilst inviting us to move beyond tools to work with our brilliance and shared humanity in order to achieve profound insight, learning and change. The 7Cs can support our work with clients and help us to attend to our own personal and professional development. WHO we are is HOW we work.

I have increasingly found that whilst competencies, models and expertise are important they can only take us so far in working effectively with people in today's global world of constant volatility and complex unpredictability.

Instead, I have become fascinated by how, as practitioners, we can learn to embrace our own humanity and our shared human condition to embrace that of others. This is where the true spirit of insight, creativity, learning and change lies, and from here we can role model this for our clients. I also found myself discovering that working in this way was the difference, which was making THE difference. I am also very much work in progress!

I found myself agreeing with John Naisbitt when he wrote[2]:

> The most exciting breakthroughs in the twenty-first century will not occur because of technology but because of an expanding concept of what it means to be human.

# Section 2
## Origins of the 7Cs

# Section 2
## Origins of the 7Cs

This new lens emerged in me – and for me – whilst I was walking up in the Lake District in the summer of 2017.

I had been working on my new book – *Reflect to Create! The Dance of Reflection for Creative Leadership and Professional Practice* – which is now out[3].

One of the headlines from my research had been that reflection was an act of creativity. I had found that reflection was the learning process, which brings the new into the world – be it a new idea, a new design, a new mindset, a new offer, a new product or a new way of being, relating or working. At the same time I started to notice that competency checklists – whilst invaluable – were no longer inspiring me. I also sensed that creativity is natural and innate in us because we are human.

So on my walk I started to ask myself, given that Creativity is an innate human quality, what other qualities had I observed which were also important to me? What then came to me were the 7Cs of Care, Courage, Curiosity, Compassion, Connection, Creativity and Contemplation. I immediately recognized these as the heart-based capacities and qualities which supported me and held me to account. I also knew that without these capacities and qualities I – and my work – become quickly denuded and impoverished.

I have since road tested this lens whenever I have felt challenged, lost my mojo, felt stuck, or needed some inspiration to help my clients reconnect with their own innate brilliance. I have also found that each of the 7Cs can feed and complement the others in surprising and unexpected ways.

The beauty of the 7Cs is that they are all innate heart-based human qualities. They are therefore naturally available to us – if we choose them – at any time. They also offer a lens which can be used for exploring WHO we are and WHO we are becoming and HOW this shows up in us, in our relationships and in our work as we work. The 7Cs can be used to inform the quality of our practice as well as support our own personal and professional development. The 7Cs put us at the frontier field of our shared humanity in order to enrich ourselves and deepen our work.

# Section 3
## Defining the 7Cs

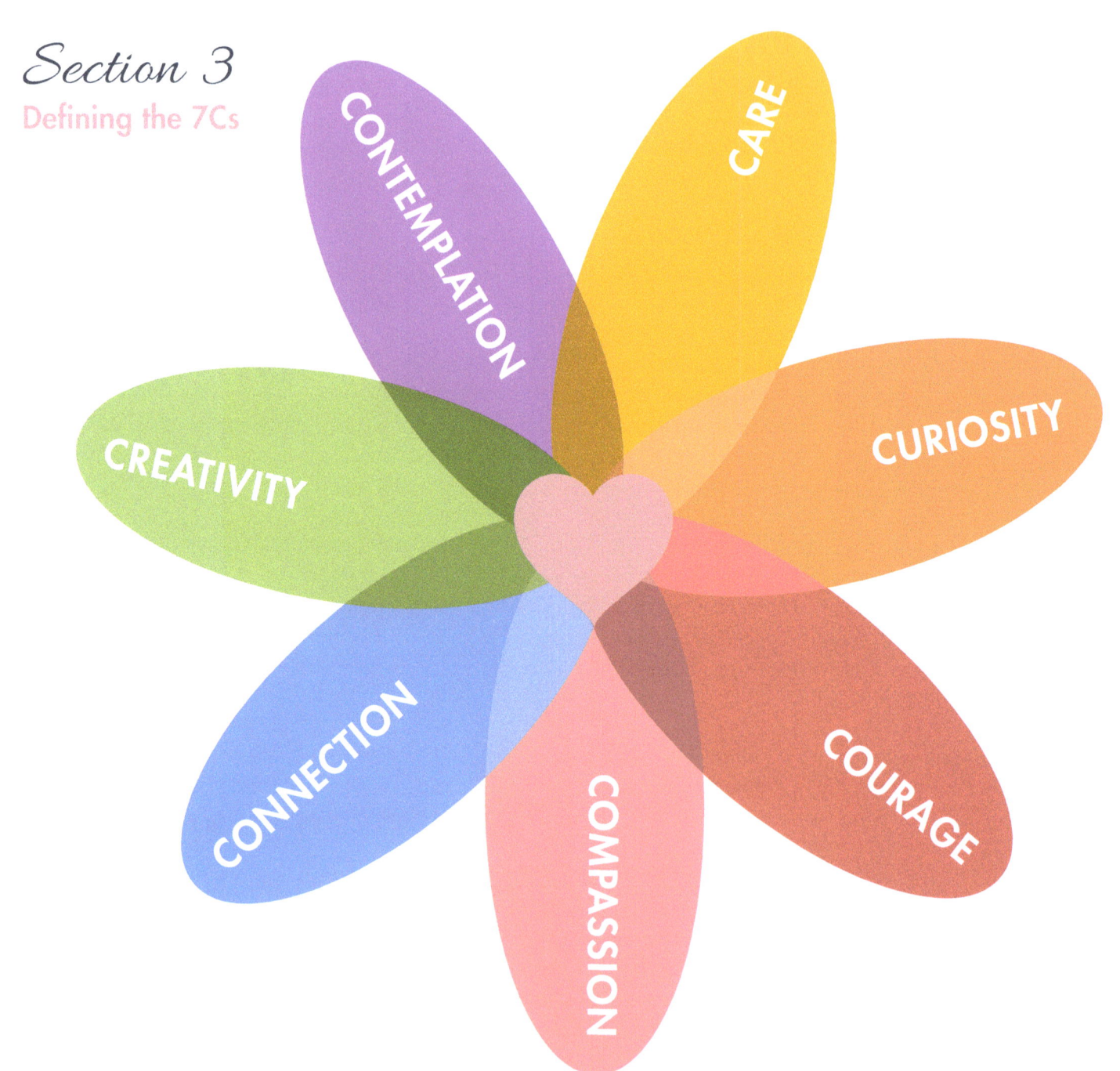

# Section 3
## Defining the 7Cs

The 7Cs are our 7 human capacities or qualities for Care, **Courage**, **Curiosity**, **Compassion**, **Connection**, **Creativity** and **Contemplation**. They have been selected because:

- **Care** is at the heart of our being human. What and who we care about, and how, defines us
- **Courage** is the capacity of the heart to speak its truth and to be brave, bold, vulnerable and wise
- **Curiosity** and our natural inquisitiveness - allows us to expand our learning
- **Compassion** helps us to see the inter-relatedness of all of life, to connect to the feelings of others whilst staying centred and connected to our true selves
- **Connection** helps us to see the deeper underlying essence of all of life – the whole of which we are all a part
- **Creativity** helps us to break old ways of thinking, relating and seeing while spawning fresh approaches to life
- **Contemplation** is making the time to turn to tune into ourselves, to be with ourselves and hear ourselves think and feel.

Each quality will be described and defined in greater detail, together with key inquiries to help bring each quality alive. The journey starts with embracing our own vulnerability and humanity.

Our work together is to explore how you can bring more of these qualities to life for yourself, your teams and your work. Journaling as you work through the 7 capacities is a very helpful way to capture your deeper reflections and inquiries. A reflective self-assessment map is provided at the end of this section to help you to identify the capacities and qualities which you would like to invite into your life.

# Section 4
## Working with the 7Cs

### CARE

# *Capacity 1*
# Care

## Definition

Caring is at the heart of being and at the heart of our humanity. Passion is over-rated and cannot always be sustained. What and who we care about, and how, defines us.

Caring (and taking care) with people, issues, choices and decisions is actually the fundamental expression of our deeper purpose. It is our values and integrity in action. It is also how we are experienced by others. Caring sets the compass for authentic, ethical and compassionate leadership and professional practice. The work is relational. Trust has to be earned. It is not given automatically. As Ken Cashman writes[4]:

> Leadership – and professional practice – is not simply something we do. It comes from somewhere inside us... and it is a process, an intimate expression of who we are.
> It is our being in action.

## Reflective Questions

Core Questions to explore this capacity in you or with your clients are:

- What do you truly and fundamentally care about?
- Why do you choose to lead or practice?
- Do you care enough about this?
- Is this decision ethical?
- How care-full are you? On a scale of 0 to 10 where 0 is not at all and 10 is care-full all of the time or when I need to be, where would you place yourself?

## Your Reflections

# CURIOSITY

# Capacity 2
## Curiosity

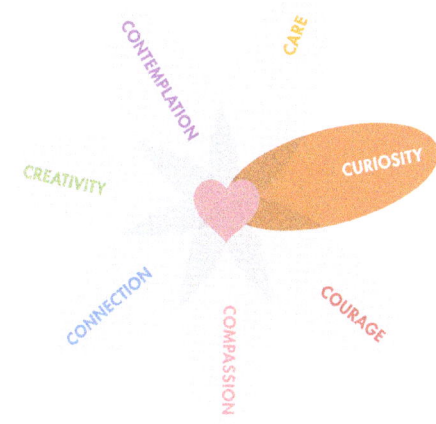

### Definition

Curiosity's natural inquisitiveness drives inquiry, questioning and learning. Curiosity keeps leaders and people practitioners open and receptive. The human brain loves questions. Curiosity keeps us awake and alert to our blind spots. It avoids complacency, questions the status quo and drives creativity and innovation.

Curiosity's questioning puts us at the edge of our learning, challenging the known, assumed and expert to explore other possibilities, perspectives and potential; to sense and lean into what is wanting and needing to emerge. As Albert Einstein wrote[5]:

> The important thing is to not stop questioning. Curiosity has its own reason for existence.
> One cannot help but be in awe when he contemplates the mysteries
> of eternity, of life, of the marvelous structure of reality.

### Reflective Questions

Core Questions to explore this capacity in you or with your clients are:

- What are you curious about?
- When was the last time you were truly surprised or discovered something new?
- Where are your blocks or blind spots?
- What is emerging?
- Who can give you honest feedback?
- How curious are you? On a scale of 0 to 10 where 0 is not at all and 10 is curious all of the time or whenever I need to be, where would you place yourself?

## Your Reflections

# COURAGE

# Capacity 3
## Courage

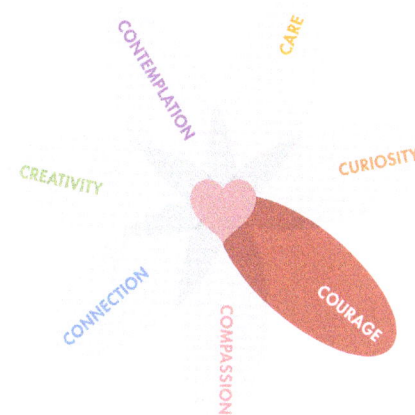

### Definition

Courage in English is derived from 'coeur', which means 'heart' in French. Courage comes from the intelligence of the heart to be brave, bold and fearless for wise action.

Courage enables us to move forward whilst also being aware of our vulnerabilities, fears and risks. Leaders with courage feel the future and act upon it, comfortable to prototype and test and learn. According to Coco Chanel[6]:

> The most courageous act is still to think for yourself. Aloud.

### Reflective Questions

Core Questions to explore this capacity in you or with your clients are:

- What I am called to do?
- What I am here for?
- What do I really want to create in my life?
- How courageous are you? On a scale of 0 to 10 where 0 is not at all and 10 is courageous all of the time or whenever I need to be, where would you place yourself?

**Your Reflections**

# COMPASSION

# Capacity 4
## Compassion

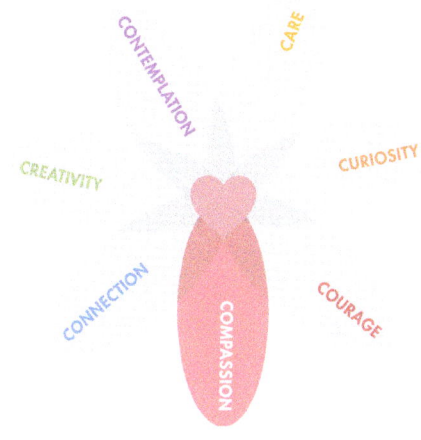

### Definition

Compassion is the capacity to connect with yourself, with others and with our shared humanity, with loving kindness. Compassion is not just empathy. Compassion is the capacity to be with, to connect to the feelings of others whilst also staying centred and connected to self. Compassion is the awareness of the interrelatedness of everything. People exist in relation to each other. Compassion is the capacity to embrace all of what it means to be fully human with loving kindness: the vulnerabilities, the joys, the losses and the celebrations, which accompany an everyday life. Self-compassion is when we are also able to extend that gift to ourselves. In 1624, the poet John Donne wrote[7]:

> No man is an island, Entire of itself, Every man is a piece of the continent, A part of the main. If a clod be washed away by the sea, Europe is the less. As well as if a promontory were. As well as if a manor of thy friend's Or of thine own were: Any man's death diminishes me, Because I am involved in mankind, And therefore never send to know for whom the bell tolls; It tolls for thee.

### Reflective Questions

Core Questions to explore this capacity in you or with your clients are:

- How do you extend your compassion to others?
- How do you extend self-compassion to yourself?
- How accepting are you of your own and others' vulnerabilities; and how do they show up in your work?
- How, who and what do you judge?
- What touched you most today?
- How compassionate are you? How self-compassionate are you? On a scale of 0 to 10 where 0 is not at all and 10 is compassionate and self-compassionate all of the time or whenever I need to be, where would you place yourself?

## Your Reflections

# CONNECTION

# Capacity 5
## Connection

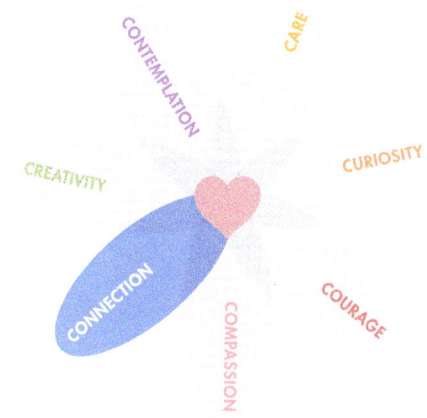

### Definition

Connection is the capacity to see the deeper underlying and universal interrelatedness in and between all of life. Connection is also the capacity to appreciate and value our own intimate relationship with all living things across the dimensions of past, present and future.

Connection gives us a bigger perspective, purpose and sense of belonging within the world and the work we do; and an awareness of how our actions can affect others and how planet. As Albert Einstein wrote[8]:

> A human being is part of the whole, called by us the 'universe', a part limited in time and space. He experiences himself, his thoughts and his feelings, as something separated from the rest, a kind of optical illusion of his consciousness. This delusion is a kind of prison for us, restricting us to our personal desires and to affection for a few persons nearest to us. Our task must be to free to ourselves from this prison by widening our circle of compassion to embrace all living creatures and the whole of nature in its beauty.

### Reflective Questions

Core Questions to explore this capacity in you or with your clients are:

- When, how and why did you last feel a deep connection with someone or something?
- What did this connection feel like?
- What happened?
- How did your perspective alter?
- How connected are you? On a scale of 0 to 10 where 0 is not at all and 10 is connected all of the time or whenever I need to be, where would you place yourself?

## Your Reflections

# CREATIVITY

# Capacity 6
## Creativity

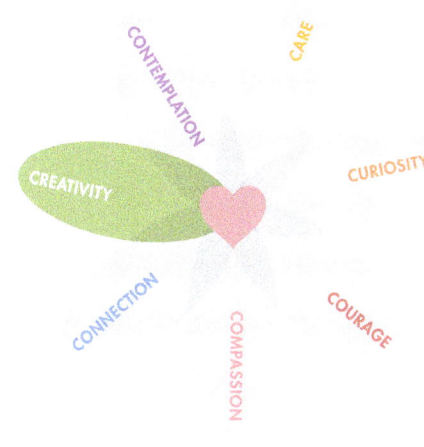

### Definition

Creativity is the capacity to break old patterns and habitual ways of being, seeing, relating, learning and working to create anew. Creativity is the capacity to bring the new into the world – be it a new product, idea, insight or way of working – whilst also being deeply respectful of past efforts, which have brought the individual or team to the point of a new creative breakthrough.

As George Lois, an American Art Director said[9]:

> Creativity can solve any problem. The creative act, the defeat of habit by originality, overcomes everything.

Creativity thrives where there is time and space for care, curiosity, courage, compassion, connection and contemplation, to blend and work their magic.

### Reflective Questions

Core Questions to explore this capacity in you or with your clients are:

- What inspires you?
- What are the seeds of the future in the present here and now?
- How can you bring more light and playfulness into your work to enable creativity to flourish?
- How creative are you? On a scale of 0 to 10 where 0 is not at all and 10 is creative all of the time or whenever I need to be, where would you place yourself?

## Your Reflections

# CONTEMPLATION

# Capacity 7
## Contemplation

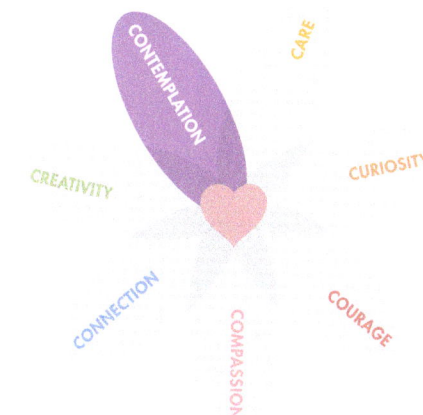

### Definition

Contemplation involves turning away from the endless busyness, rush and noise of everyday living to tune into ourselves, be with ourselves and hear ourselves think.

Contemplation is the capacity to listen deeply to ourselves; to sit with and to be with issues, trusting that in time – and with time – our own inner wisdom and knowing will surface. It is the capacity to be fully and mindfully present in the moment, which stills the ego and our strategic minds to listen to all of our other and perhaps quieter bodily, heart-based and soulful intelligences. As Parker J Palmer writes[10]:

> The soul is like a wild animal… whilst tough, resilient and resourceful, savvy and self-sufficient…
> it is also shy… and will only come out when it is safe to do so…

### Reflective Questions

Core Questions to explore this capacity in you or with your clients are:

- Do you create the time and space to tune into yourself?
- How do you listen to yourself think?
- What are you holding onto that you need to let go of, to see afresh?
- How contemplative and reflective are you? On a scale of 0 to 10 where 0 is not at all and 10 is contemplative and reflective all of the time or whenever you need to be, where would you place yourself?

**Your Reflections**

# Section 5
## Self-Assessment Map

You can use the graphic below by yourself or with your clients to identify your underlying patterns and development edges. These can then inform your personal and professional development conversations.

**Your Reflections**

# Section 6
## 7Cs in Action

# Section 6
## 7Cs in Action

**Here are some reflections from clients who have used the 7Cs.**

Inspiring and practical. A very useful reflective tool shared beautifully by the author

*2019 Coaching@Work Highly Commended Article of the Year: Panel Feedback*

This is simply a gorgeous way to consider reflection-on-practice – such a freshness and such a carefully considered process. Every one of the 7Cs lights up new territory for us to explore. Elaine Patterson is a well-informed and capable guide, and this imaginative and powerful process is a perfect companion for leaders, supervisors and coaches who want to stay open, stay fresh, enhance their professional skills and work with our shared humanity.

*Edna Murdoch, Founder and Director at the Coaching Supervision Academy Ltd.*

The 7Cs are a very comprehensive prism which puts in perspective how to work with our shared humanity, starting with oneself. The 7Cs have been a background music to my coaching and leadership practice ready to be called upon when needed

*Paul Tran, Associate at INSEAD Business School*

Earlier this year I was working with a group of experienced internal coaches helping them develop their practice in order to step into more visible roles in regional offices. Whilst we spent some considerable time developing their competencies as coaches, the real shift and deep work came by reflecting on the 7 capacities and how they related to not just 'doing' coaching but what it meant for them to 'be' coaches. Each person stood by each petal in turn to speak of how that 'C' showed up in their practice. The 7Cs formed a basis of inquiry about how they were showing up in their work, what impacted on them and contributed to highlighting their signature strengths and areas of further development. It also gave them a vocabulary to explore situations with a fresh lens with clients.

*Karyn Prentice, Fletcher Prentice Associates*

It has been amazing to note how 7Cs human capabilities form a necklace of precious stones, unique and in absolute harmony. I have been transformed in each immersion in this necklace! I have also been using the 7Cs in my role as coach supervisor, both in individual and group sessions, as well as in a conference for around 100 coaches, managers and leaders in Bahia-Brazil, with a central theme of active listening in leadership and self-leadership. In this context, the 7Cs resonated as a deep level of development that broadens listening fields for greater synchronicity in 'we and us together' capabilities to connect, create and broaden emerging and transforming possibilities for a better whole.

*Clenir Streit, International Coaching and Consulting, Rio Grande do Sul, Brazil*

The 7Cs Being Fully Human convey both the gentleness of their intentions and the powerful impact they can unleash. Mapping the navigation and exploration of coaching and coaching supervision with this new lens brings both grace and gravitas to the conversations. The beauty of the 7Cs lies in their apparent simplicity. As a practitioner I find them to be the pillars on which I can rest my inner supervisor and for my clients to be the base of their authentic leadership. Very specifically, either in the course of a session or while reviewing it, I now use the 7Cs as a checklist for my professional posture, for the relationship with the client, for the client him/herself and for the system in which she/he operates.

*Edith Coron PCC-ICF, CSA Supervisor, France*

I have been using Elaine Patterson's 7 Cs cards for a year now. I have found them very inspiring and useful to both my executive coaching practice and my clients. In self-supervision, it allows me to re-focus on what is important for me at a moment in time and helps me to clear out some of the issues I might have with my clients. Being drawn to a specific card when reflecting on a situation helps me see parallel process or blind spots. In individual coaching I use them in various ways. What I like is that I can pull them out when I feel it is helpful for my clients and it's always at different moments or for different reasons. For example, I closed a session by asking my client which card she would choose that best reflects her learnings from the session, that has helped her understand what she was focusing on but was enable to express. Another example, I asked a client to think of a member of his team he was having difficulties with and choose the cards that best described his relationship with that person. That helped him realize where the issue was coming from, it helped him clarify what was in the way, and he then understood very quickly what he needed to do to work better with that person.

*Caroline Hercz, CEO and Executive Coach at Human Place, Paris*

I have used this model with 5 clients to date, and in a variety of different ways. It has landed with every client I have used it with, including clients who brought issues to sessions (e.g. What C might help with this? What C could use topping up? etc.), as well as clients who do not have an issue as such but have used the 7Cs to open a discussion that brings about identification of new goals. Having the individual petals on the table encourages the client to move them around, pick them up and create links between them, which adds a kinaesthetic element to the tool. I believe that welcoming a client into a room with the beautiful, colourful petals already laid out creates a welcoming atmosphere, and invites the client to bring their curiosity about what we might be doing, which really gathers their attention! Overall, I love it! Thank you so much for sharing this with me, and us as a Trust. It fits so well with our values as an organisation and I know that this will be a well-used model for many years to come!

Hannah Datema, Coaching and Mentoring Development Manager,
NHS London Teaching Trust

# Section 7
## References, Further Resources and Reading

# Section 7
## References, Further Resources and Reading

### References

[1] Patterson, E. (2015) *'What are leaders' experiences of reflection?'* What leaders and leadership developers need to know from the findings of an exploratory research study, Reflective Practice, Volume 16 Number 5, pp 636-651 [Internet] http://dx.doi.org/10.1080/14623943.2015.1064386

[2] Naisbitt, J. quoted in Laloux, F. (2014) *Reinventing Organizations: A Guide to Creating Organizations Inspired by the Next Stage in Human Consciousness.* Pp 43. Belgium, Nelson Parker

[3] Patterson, E. (2019) *Reflect to Create! The Dance of Reflection for Creative Leadership, Professional Practice and Supervision.* London, The Centre for Reflection and Creativity Ltd.

[4] Cashman, K. (2008) *Leadership from the Inside Out; Becoming a Leader for Life.* Pp 22. San Francisco, Berrett-Koehler Publishers Inc.

[5] Einstein, A. (1955) "Old Man's Advice to Youth: 'Never Lose a Holy Curiosity.'" Pp64 *LIFE Magazine*

[6] Karbo, K (2009) *The Gospel According to Coco Chanel: Life Lessons from the World's Most Elegant Woman.* London, Skirt

[7] Donne, J. (1624) "Devotions upon Emergent Occasions", Meditation XVII. From *The Works of John Donne.* vol III. Henry Alford, ed. London: John W. Parker, 1839. 574-5

[8] Calaprice, A. (2005) *The New Quotable Einstein.* Pp 206. USA, Princeton University Press

[9] Christensen, T. (2015) *The Creativity Challenge.* Pp 5. Avon, Adams Media

[10] Palmer, P. (2008) *A Hidden Wholeness: The Journey Toward An Undivided Life.* Pp 58. San Francisco, John Wiley and Sons, Inc.

# Further Resources and Reading

## Capacity 1: Care

Brown, J. with Issacs, D. (2005) *The World Café – Shaping our Futures through Conversations that Matter.* San Francisco, Berrett-Koehler Publishers

Dalai Lama and van den Muyzenberg, L. (2008) *The Leaders Way.* London, Nicholas Brealey Publishing

Dalai Lama (2011) *A Profound Mind – Cultivating Wisdom in Everyday Life.* London, Hodder & Stoughton

Giono, J. (1995) *The Man Who Planted Tress.* Massachusetts, Shambhala Publications Ltd.

Goleman, D. (2013) Focus: *The Hidden Driver of Excellence.* London, Bloomsbury Publishing Plc.

Greenleaf, R. K. (2002) *Servant Leadership – A Journey into the Nature of Legitimate Power and Greatness.* 3rd ed. New Jersey, Paulist Press Ltd.

Huffington, A. (2014) *Thrive The Third Metric to Redefining Success and Creating and Happier Life.* USA, Harmony Books

Hutchins, G. (2012) *The Nature of Business – Redesigning Business for Resilience.* Devon, Green Books Ltd.

Hutchins, G. (2016) *Future Fit.* Self published

Laloux, F. (2014) *Reinventing Organizations: A Guide to Creating Organizations Inspired by the Next Stage in Human Consciousness.* Belgium, Nelson Parker

O'Neill, M. (2000) *Executive Coaching with Backbone and Heart.* Chichester, John Wiley & Son

Pellicer, L., O., (2008) *Caring Enough to Lead: How Reflective practice Leads to Moral Leadership.* 3rd ed. Thousand Oaks, SAGE Publications

Szpakowski, S. (2010) *Little Book of Practice for Authentic Leadership in Action.* Canada, the ALIA Institute

Steare, R. (2011) *Ethicability® (n) How to Decide What's Right and Find the Courage to Do It.* UK: Roger Steare Consulting Ltd.

## Capacity 2: Curiosity

Kline, N. (1999) *Time to Think: Listening to Ignite the Human Mind.* London, Ward Lock

Palmer, P. J. (2000) *Let Your Life Speak – Listening for the Voice of Vocation.* San Francisco, Jossey-Bass

Palmer, P.J. (1990) *The Active Life – A Spirituality of Work, Creativity and Caring.* San Francisco, Jossey-Bass

Richo, D. (2017) *The Five Longings: What We Have Always Wanted and Already Have – A Guide to Love, Meaning, Freedom, Happiness and Growth.* Colorado, Shambhala Publications Ltd

Shohet, R. Ed. (2011) *Supervision as Transformation – A Passion for Learning.* London, Jessica Kingsley Publishers

Whyte, D. (2001) *Crossing the Unknown Sea: Work as a Pilgrimage of Identity.* New York, Riverhead Books

Whyte, D. (1994) *The Heart Aroused Poetry and the Preservation of the Soul in the Workplace.* New York, Random House

## Capacity 3: Courage

Brown, B. (2010) *The Gifts of Imperfection: Let Go of Who You Think You're Supposed to Be and Embrace Who You Are. Your Guide to Wholehearted Living.* Minnesota, Hazelden

Brown, B. (2012) *Daring Greatly How the Courage to Be Vulnerable Transforms the Way We Live, Love, Parent and Lead.* Penguin Group, London

Chodron, P. (2016) *When Things Fall Apart Heart Advice for Difficult Times.* Boulder,

Shambhala

## Capacity 4: Compassion

Chodron, P. (1994) *Start With Where You Are: How to Accept Yourself and Others.* London, HarperCollins Publishers

Chodron, P. (2001) *Start Where You Are: A Guide to Compassionate Living.* USA, Shambhala Publications

Fredrickson, B. (2014) *Love 2:0.* New York, Penguin

Germer, G. (2009) *The Mindful Path to Self Compassion.* New York, The Guildford Press

Lewis, T., Amini, F. & Lannon, R. (2001) *A General Theory of Love.* New York, Random House

Neff, K. (2011) *Self Compassion Stop Beating Yourself Up and Leave Insecurity Behind.* Hodder and Stoughton Ltd, London

Salzberg, Sh. (2002) *Loving Kindness – The Revolutionary Art of Happiness.* Massachusetts, Shambhala Publications

## Capacity 5: Connection

Buber, M. (1958) I and Thou. New York, The Scribner Library.

Carr, N. (2010) *The Shallows – How the Internet is Changing the Way We Think, Read and Remember.* New York, W.W. Norton & Company Inc.

de Haan, E. (2008) *Relational Coaching.* Chichester, John Wiley.

Hutchins, G. (2014) *The Illusion of Separation – Exploring the Cause of our Current Crisis.* Edinburgh, Floris Books.

Jaworski, J. (2011) *Synchronicity – The Inner Path to Leadership.* San Francisco, Berrett-Koehler Publishers.

Kline, N. (1999) *Time to Think: Listening to Ignite the Human Mind.* London, Ward Lock

McTaggart, L. (2001) *The Field.* London, HarperCollins Publishers

Parlett, M. (2015) *Future Sense – Five Explorations of Whole Intelligence for a World That's Waking Up.* Leicestershire, Matador Books

Rozenthuler, S. (2012) *Life-Changing Conversations – 7 Strategies for Talking About What Matters Most.* London, Watkins Publishing

Scharmer, O. & Kaufer, K. (2013) *Leading from the Emerging Future: From Ego-System to Eco-System Economies: Applying Theory U to Transforming Business, Society, and Self.* San Francisco, Berrett-Koehler Publishers, Inc.

Senge, P., Scharmer, O., Jaworski, J., and Flowers, B. S. (2005) *Presence – Exploring Profound Change in People, Organisations and Society.* London, Nicholas Brealey Publishing

Siegel, D. (2010) *Mindsight: Transform your Brain with the New Science of Kindness.* London, Oneworld Publications

Siegel, D. (2015) *The Developing Mind – How Relationships and the Brain Interact to Shape Who we Are.* New York, Guildford Press

Turkle, S. (2015) *Reclaiming Conversation – The Power of Talk in a Digital Age.* New York, Penguin Press

Wolinsky, S. (1993) *Quantum Consciousness: The Guide to Experiencing Quantum Psychology.* Canada, Bramble Books

Zohar, D. and Marsall, I. (2000) *Spiritual Intelligence: The Ultimate Intelligence.* London, Bloomsbury Publishing Plc

## Capacity 6: Creativity

Bohm, D. (1996) *On Creativity*. Oxon, Routledge

Cameron, J. (1994) *The Artists Way – A Course in Discovering and Recovering Your Creative Self*. London, Pan Books

Cameron, J. (1996) *The Vein of Gold – A Journey to Your Creative Heart*. USA, Tarcher/Putman

Cameron, J. (2016) *It's Never Too Late to Begin Again – Discovering Creativity and Meaning at Midlife and Beyond*. New York, TarcherPerigree

Christensen, T. (2015) *The Creativity Challenge*. MA, Adams Media

Fox, M. (2002) *Creativity – Where the Divine and Human Meet*. New York, Tarcher/Putman Books

Gilbert, E. (2015) *Big Magic – Creative Living Beyond Fear*. London, Bloomsbury Publishing

Gompertz, W. (2015) *Think Like An Artist… and Lead a More Creative, Productive Life*. UK, Penguin Random House

Judkins, R. (2015) *The Art of Creative Thinking*. London, Hodder & Stoughton Ltd

May, R. (1975) *The Courage to Create*. New York, W.W. Norton & Company

Osho (1999) *Creativity: Unleashing the Forces Within*. New York, Osho International Foundation

Penman, D. (2015) *Mindfulness for Creativity. Adapt, Create and Thrive in a Frantic World*. London, Piatkus

Udall, N. (2014) *Riding the Creative Rollercoaster: How Leaders Evoke Creativity, Productivity and Innovation*. London, Kogan Page

Udall, N. and Turner, N. (2008) *The Way of Nowhere – 8 Questions to Release Our Creative Potential*. London, HarperCollins Publishers

Ulrich, D. (2002) *The Widening Stream – The Seven Stages of Creativity*. Pp ix. Oregan, Beyond Words Publishing Inc

Design by Kelly Alderdice at 2Ten Graphic Design / Editing by Emma Dickens

## Capacity 7: Contemplation

Brown, J. (2006) *Reflective Practices for Transformational Leaders.* futureAge May/June 2006

Brown, J. (2008) *A Leader's Guide to Reflective Practice.* USA, Trafford Publishing

Frankl, V. (1959) *Man's Search for Meaning – The Classic Tribute to Hope in the Holocaust.* London, Rider

Gendlin, E. (1978) *Focusing.* New York, Bantam Dell

Gilligan, S. and Dilts, R. (2009) *The Hero's Journey: A Voyage of Self Discovery.* Carmarthen, Crown House Publishing Ltd

Harris, M. (2017) *Solitude – In Pursuit of a Singular Life in a Crowded World.* London, Random House Books

Hillman, J. (1996) *The Souls Code: In Search of Character and Calling.* New York, Grand Central Publishing

Intrator, S. & Scribner, M. (2007) *Leading from Within – Poetry That Sustains the Courage to Lead.* San Francisco, Jossey-Bass

Kabat-Zinn, J. (1994) *Where You Go, There You Are – Mindfulness Meditation for Everyday Life.* London, Little, Brown Book Group

Kabat-Zinn, J. (2005) *Coming to our Senses.* New York, Hyperion Press

O'Donahue, J. (2008) *To Bless the Space Between Us: A Book of Blessings.* USA, Sounds True Inc

O'Donohue, J. (1998) *Anam Cara: A Book of Celtic Wisdom.* New York, Harper Perennial

Whyte, D. (2015) *Consolations: The Solace, Nourishment and Underlying Meaning of Everyday Words.* Langley, Many Rivers Press

Salvation of this human world lies nowhere else than in the human heart
– in the human power to reflect, in human meekness and human responsibility

Vaclav Havel

## NOTES

www.ingramcontent.com/pod-product-compliance
Lightning Source LLC
Chambersburg PA
CBHW042036100526
44587CB00030B/4457